Little **BIG** Chats

Mindfulness

by Jayneen Sanders

illustrated by Cherie Zamazing

Mindfulness
Educate2Empower Publishing an imprint of
UpLoad Publishing Pty Ltd
Victoria Australia
www.upload.com.au

First published in 2021

Written by Jayneen Sanders
Illustrations by Cherie Zamazing

Jayneen Sanders asserts her right to be identified as the author of this work.
Cherie Zamazing asserts her right to be identified as the illustrator of this work.

Designed by Stephanie Spartels, Studio Spartels

ISBN: 9781761160219 (hbk) 9781761160073 (pbk)

A catalogue record for this
book is available from the
National Library of Australia

Disclaimer: The information in this book is advice only, written by the author based on
her advocacy in this area, and her experience working with children as a classroom teacher
and mother. The information is not meant to be a substitute for professional advice. If you
are concerned about a child's behavior seek professional help.

Using Little **BIG** Chats

The *Little BIG Chats* series has been written to assist parents, caregivers and educators to have open and age-appropriate conversations with young children around crucial, and yet at times, 'tough' topics. And what better way than using children's picture books! Some pages will have questions for your child to interact with and discuss. Feel free to use these questions and the Discussion Questions provided on page 19 of this book to help you assist your child with the topic being explored. Stop at any time to unpack the text together; and try to follow your child's lead wherever that conversation may take you! So, please, get comfy and start some empowering 'chats' around some BIG topics with your child.

The Body Safety titles should ideally be read in the following order:
Consent, *My Safety Network*, *My Early Warning Signs*,
Private Parts are Private, and *Secrets and Surprises*.
The remaining titles can be read in any order.

Meet the

Little **BIG** Chats
KIDS

Theodore

Asha

Ardie

Tom

Jun

Jamie

Belle

Lisa

Maisy

Tilly

Maya

Ben

Hi! I'm Maisy.
Today we're learning
about being calm
and enjoying each day.

Mindfulness is
spending time quietly.

It is taking time to
notice the things
around you.

It is taking time
to be calm.

DO YOU KNOW WHAT CALM MEANS?

Mindfulness is really helpful if your mind is full of busy thoughts, or you are worried or scared.

When I feel this way,
I find a quiet place to sit.

Then I close my eyes.

I breathe in slowly 1, 2, 3.

And I breathe out slowly 4, 5, 6.

I keep doing this until I feel calm.

WOULD YOU LIKE
TO TRY THIS?

WHAT CAN
YOU HEAR?

11

Sometimes I sit quietly,
close my eyes and imagine
a beautiful garden.

I imagine walking through
my special garden.

There are so many things to see!

My garden is always changing.

WHAT DOES YOUR GARDEN LOOK LIKE?

MAYBE YOU MIGHT LIKE TO DRAW YOUR GARDEN.

13

I love to walk on the beach with my dad.

We take our time.

We listen to the ocean.

We watch the birds flying over the waves.

We smell the salty air.

We feel the sand between our toes.

This is mindfulness too!

WOULD YOU LIKE TO
TRY THIS WITH A
TRUSTED GROWN-UP?

MAYBE YOU COULD
WALK IN A FOREST.

My dad taught me
some yoga poses.

I do these to stretch my
body and calm my mind.

I do slow breathing
when I do my yoga poses.

Breathe in 1, 2, 3.

Breathe out 4, 5, 6.

Slow breathing
calms me down.

WOULD YOU LIKE
TO TRY THESE
YOGA POSES?

Mindfulness is very important.

It helps us to calm our mind.

It helps us to look and listen.

It helps us to notice the world around us.

WHAT CAN YOU SEE AROUND YOU?

DISCUSSION QUESTIONS
for Parents, Caregivers and Educators

The following Discussion Questions are intended as a guide, and can be used to initiate open, age-appropriate and empowering conversations with your child.

This book is a simple introduction to mindfulness. During challenging times, children can feel quite anxious. Learning mindfulness techniques from a young age will help them build resilience and reduce anxiety and stress as they grow into adulthood.

Page 5
Introduce Maisy. Ask, 'What did you do today? Did you enjoy your day?'

Pages 6-7
Ask, 'Have you heard of mindfulness before? What do you think it means? Let's look around us. What can you see/hear/smell/touch/feel? What or who makes you feel calm?'

Pages 8-9
Ask, 'What do you think is going on for Maisy in these pictures? What kind of busy thoughts do you have? How might mindfulness help you with your busy or worrying thoughts?'

Pages 10-11
Say, 'Let's try some mindfulness.' Have you and your child sit quietly like Maisy. Now close your eyes and breathe in 1, 2, 3 and breathe out 4, 5, 6 slowly. Repeat. Ask, 'How are you feeling now? What did you hear or smell? What is a good word to describe how you are feeling?'

Pages 12-13
You can use this page as a guided meditation. Ask your child to sit quietly and comfortably, and close their eyes. Ask them to imagine a beautiful garden; their own special garden where there are red and blue butterflies ... continue with descriptions for the child. Alternatively, have your child sit quietly for five minutes and imagine their own garden that they can later describe to you. If they wish to they can draw either garden.

Pages 14-15
Ask, 'How is Maisy being mindful at the beach? Do you like going to the beach? What things do you like to do? How might you be mindful at the beach? How might you be mindful in a forest?' Note: if children find going to sleep difficult because of worries or busy thoughts, you could ask, 'How might mindfulness help you when you go to sleep?'

Pages 16-17
Ask, 'What is yoga?' If your child doesn't know anything about yoga, explain that yoga consists of exercises for your body but because they are done slowly, while also breathing slowly, they help to calm your mind too!

Page 18
Ask, 'Why do you think it is important to have a calm mind?' Invite your child to go outside with you. Sit in a quiet place. Ask, 'What can you see/hear/smell/touch/feel?'

For more books on mindfulness, see Jayneen Sanders' children's books 'I'm Calm' and 'Hey There! What's Your Superpower?'.

Little BIG Chats

A series of 12 little books to help kids unpack BIG topics

Consent
Introducing consent and body boundaries

by Jayneen Sanders   Illustrated by Cherie Zamazing

Secrets and Surprises
Learning the difference between secrets and surprises

by Jayneen Sanders   Illustrated by Cherie Zamazing

Private Parts are Private
Learning private parts are private and what to do if touched inappropriately

by Jayneen Sanders   Illustrated by Cherie Zamazing

My Safety Network
Introducing a Safety Network (3 to 5 trusted adults a child can go to if they feel unsafe)

by Jayneen Sanders   Illustrated by Cherie Zamazing

My Early Warning Signs
Exploring Early Warning Signs and what to do if a child experiences these signs

by Jayneen Sanders   Illustrated by Cherie Zamazing

Families
Celebrating diversity in families

by Jayneen Sanders   Illustrated by Cherie Zamazing

I Always Try
Developing a growth mindset of resilience and persistence

by Jayneen Sanders   Illustrated by Cherie Zamazing

Feelings
Understanding different feelings and emotions

by Jayneen Sanders   Illustrated by Cherie Zamazing

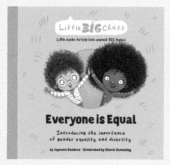

Everyone is Equal
Introducing the importance of gender equality and diversity

by Jayneen Sanders   Illustrated by Cherie Zamazing

Empathy
Exploring the meaning of empathy and kindness

by Jayneen Sanders   Illustrated by Cherie Zamazing

Mindfulness
Exploring the importance of mindfulness and learning calming skills

by Jayneen Sanders   Illustrated by Cherie Zamazing

Around the World
Celebrating racial equality and diversity

by Jayneen Sanders   Illustrated by Cherie Zamazing

CPSIA information can be obtained
at www.ICGtesting.com
Printed in the USA
LVHW071116290123
738162LV00013B/730

9 781761 160219